Praises
Prepare For

D0933108

"Prepare For The Wolf" is an excellent ... ... ing skills and is perfect for character education training and leadership curriculum. Robert Roots is a role model among role models. We are proud to have him as a consultant for our School System.

Anthony Rolle, Director Career Education, Miami Dade County Public Schools

It truly only takes a minute to change your life. Take a minute, read "Prepare For The Wolf" and discover that it is possible to turn setbacks into incredible comebacks.

Willie Jolley, Author, "A Setback is a setup for a Comeback"

A motivational book which describes human behavior through a fable. "Prepare for the Wolf" places the reader on a road to self-analysis and empowerment.

Gil Suarez, V.P. Lakewood H.S., N.J.

My expectation before reading this book was high because of my business relationship with the author, Robert Roots, but he managed to exceed even that. Inspiring.

Rovel L.C. Morris, C.E.O. Bridgetown Cruise Terminals, Inc. Barbados

Straw People, Wood People, Brick People, the Wolf. I love it.

Dr. Tina "The Chicken Lady" Dupree, Author, Speaker, Radio Host

Whoever thought "The Three Little Pigs" meant so much about success. If you have a youth or young adult in your home or organization, this book is essential.

Prof. Dr. Donald Jones, University of Miami

Additional Praises for
Prepare For The Wolf

This book is a fantastic asset for educators, clergy, parents and youth to invision and EXACT a brighter future. Choose to catch the spirit and "Prepare for the Wolf," an always relevant message.

W. Steven Green, Liaison, Florida Department of Education

Challenge and teach yourself how to overcome adversity and take control of your life. "Prepare For The Wolf" is deep in nature, yet simplistic in concept making it a wonderful read for both young and old.

Patrick Bowman, CEO Bowman Consulting

"Prepare For The Wolf" is a book about life, choices, consequences and personal accountability. A must for people of all ages.

Rhonda Jordan, President/Founder, Jordan Enterprises

Incredibly insightful. So valuable this book needs to be translated into every language and a copy placed in every library.

Vera Gilford, Author, "How I Broke The Glass Ceiling"

Buy my dad's book. He's a great dad and the book is great too.
Robert, Janara, Michael and Emmanuel Roots

PREPARE FOR THE WOLF

Success Secrets From The Three Little Pigs

Roots Publishing

New York

Roots Publishing
1199 Cecil Court, Suite #102
Lakewood, New Jersey 08701
732-905-5860

Book Edited by
Dawn Marie Daniels

Cover Design, Web site and Layout
Michael Valdez, www.Fastnickel.com

Author's Photo by
Benny Montanez, BM Film

Library of Congress Catalog Number: 2001099108

International Standard Book Number- 0-9715336-0-1

Printed in the United States of America

First Printing, January 2002

Dedication

This book is dedicated to my mother, Bernadette Gonzales, who taught us the value of God, love, family, courage, compassion, character and so much more.

From being a foster child under the care of New York Foundling Hospital to her last employer being the New York Foundling Hospital, where she cared for children and served as a counselor for families in crisis; my mother's life came full circle.

A divorced mother raising four children in a N.Y.C. housing project without any financial or emotional support, Mom dedicated her life to her children and to helping our numerous neighbors who were also living under similar conditions.

Though Mom's life was short, her contributions to the community and the list of people she cared for is long. From the homeless people for whom mom carried food to work with her on the subway so that she could feed them, to elderly people needing attention, to teenagers in crisis, to our relatives whom left their kids with us, at times for many months; Mom always gave to others even when it meant neglecting her own needs.

Born May 07, 1944 and gone October 03, 1994, Bernadette Gonzales' life lives on through her children; my siblings, Lorraine, Denise and Kevin, and her grandchildren, Andrea, Robert, Bernadette, Alexandra, Janara, Kaliym, Angelisa, Michael, Thalia and Emmanuel; and the many lives she has touched.

Special Acknowledgements

Special Thanks to my Aunt **Dolores Johnson**, for unselfishly contributing to my life and to all around her. Without her, my life would not have been complete.

Also to **Patricia Mellerson** for being a second mother. Though we met during a time of mutual loss, God blessed us with each other.

And **Dawn Daniels** for her friendship and adding her wisdom as an editor by helping me to find my voice.

Thank you.

To get the most from this book:

a) Read each section twice before moving on to the next section.

b) Highlight important ideas and write them down.

c) Review "Prepare for the Wolf" each month.

d) Have fun with the book. Determine if you're making Straw, Wood or Brick decisions.

e) You reap what you sow. Give copies of this book to those who you know could benefit.

f) Make a list of your goals, devise a strategy and set deadlines.

g) Learn and Master the Seven C's of Success.

h) Watch your words and conversations. Your mouth is the master key to your destiny!

i) Remember you are **Brick**. Start living like it.

"...it is in this whole process of meeting and solving problems that life has it's meaning. Problems are the cutting edge that distinguishes between success and failure. Problems call forth our courage and our wisdom; indeed, they create our courage and our wisdom. It is only because of problems that we grow mentally and spiritually... It is through the pain of confronting and resolving problems that we learn."

M. Scott Peck

TABLE OF Contents

Real Life or Folk Story?

Each year millions of people hear or read about *The Three Little Pigs*. It's taught in schools, at home, and there have been many plays and cartoons depicting the story. Yet few people understand how it applies to real life. Like many other folk stories it has primarily been used for entertainment. Though with critical evaluation one discovers that *The Three Little Pigs* is truly a metaphor for life. It's really about choices and about preparing for obstacles and challenges in life.

The material each pig chose to build their homes with represents their mind-set, Straw, Wood or Brick. These are not just materials chosen by the three pigs, we as people also build our lives out of these very same materials. The homes the pigs live in represents your life or the end result of those choices. And the Wolf is a metaphor for the obstacles and challenges we experience in life.

Most experts suggest if you want to succeed at a given goal or task, you should envision what you want to accomplish or where you want to end up before getting started. I agree, but there is another important factor to consider. If you want to reach a destination, not only is it important to know where you are going, it is equally important to know your starting point or mind-set.

Discovering which mind-set you resemble most, Straw, Wood or Brick, will help you to better understand where you are, the quality of choices you are making and will provide some foresight and insight to where you will eventually end up if you continue following the path that you are on.

Just like in the story, there's a phrase in boxing regarding a person's chin. This refers to your strength or integrity to deal with challenges and obstacles. Each pig thought that their chinny chin chin's could stand up to the power of the Wolf. It's usually not until facing a Wolf or obstacle that we find out whether the choices we made in life will sustain us under pressure.

Most of the obstacles or Wolves you encounter, you invite into your house or life by the choices you make. When you learn to anticipate the consequences of everything you say, do, think, as well as the quality of your friends and associates, you limit the amount of Wolves you have to deal with. Look at the Wood Pig. If he didn't let the Straw Pig in, then maybe the Wolf wouldn't have blown his house down.

The strength and integrity of your house must be decided before you start to build your future. Build your life with a solid foundation and brick building blocks so that when the Wolf comes, your dreams and hopes aren't destroyed. Unfortunately, many people live in a fantasy world, which does not include planning or preparing. They expect their lives to be perfect and problem free. The truth is, no one's life is problem free. Obstacles and challenges confront each and every one of us regardless of our backgrounds, race, gender or size of our dreams. Everything you experience is a by-product of the choices that you or someone else has made. Life is a mathematical equation; today represents the sum total of all those choices.

Expect success, but be a realistic optimist. Accept the fact that obstacles and challenges are part of life. Always have a Plan B and a Plan C. Do not wait for the Wolf to be standing at your front door huffing and puffing, threatening to blow your house down before you prepare for him. By then it may be too late. Just like the Straw and Wood Pig, your house too will be blown down leaving you running for shelter.

Maybe you've had a hard life, full of challenges and obstacles. Everybody has a story. It is you, who writes the end of your story. You can make it a happy ending or a sad one. There are endless books on people who have triumphed against the odds. Read about them. The real odds are determined in your mind. If you think you can't succeed, you won't. Believe in yourself, set goals, make a plan and take control of your life. Be conscious of the choices you make and the thoughts you allow into your mind.

Learn from challenges and disappointments, they don't just happen there is always a reason. These experiences are investments in your future. They will pay dividends later. Use the knowledge you gain to turn negatives into positives and to make better decisions. There are choices and consequences. You decide the consequences you have to deal with by the decisions you make. Life pays in exact measure. You reap what you sow. Be responsible with your decisions. They directly impact your life.

If you are waiting on others to take action for you, be prepared for a lifetime of disappointments and living someone else's dream, not yours. There is little satisfaction in life for those who do not take responsibility for their own lives. In life as it is in war, the element of surprise is one of the most effective tools to winning. By planning and preparing, you deny the Wolf the opportunity to catch you by surprise.

Remember: The Wolf is cunning, so be aware of your strengths and your weaknesses.

Straw, Wood or Brick, what are you made of?

Your life reflects your mind-set. Some people have been conditioned to believe that they cannot choose to be successful and that they have to settle for less. But each of us has the right and ability to be happy and successful. In fact, the stage we are at in life whether it is Straw, Wood or Brick is a result of how we think and make choices.

As you read about each of the three pigs, determine which one you resemble most. Write it down in the notes section of this book. Include reasons why you think you are Straw, Wood or Brick. Highlight areas in your life you need to improve in. Bear in mind that there are varying degrees for each mind-set but the basic attributes are the same.

Winning starts within. You control how you think and the quality of your life. The goal for your life should be to become Brick. Being Brick is a choice just like being Straw or Wood. Straw and Wood people can become Brick. It's just a matter of changing your mind-set and taking custody of your life. No condition in life is permanent. You decide its life span by the choices you make. Change your life by changing your mind-set.

Remember: Reality begins in your mind and then manifests itself in your life.

Straw People

Straw People

The Straw person does not plan their life. They leave everything to chance, living day-to-day, paycheck-to-paycheck. They don't expect much out of life. Some people are conditioned to believe that they are not capable of being anything but Straw. They were told that they were not good enough, nor smart enough to be Brick or even Wood. Straw doesn't consider the consequences of their actions, decisions or choice of people in their lives. They make choices based mainly on their emotions.

In school, Straw people are the non-achievers. These students are frequently absent without a legitimate reason. Their grades are usually failing and they don't seem to care about their future. They come unprepared for school. School is a social experience, not an educational one.

Straw people have the highest drop out rates, unplanned pregnancies and are frequently in physical or other types of altercations. These students are described by teachers to be the ones who are just taking up space because it's obvious by their grades, attendance, attitude, and conduct that they are not in school to learn.

Straw people are either unemployed or take the easiest job they could find. Because they tend to get paid the least money, they are usually the ones who complain the most about their salaries not being sufficient to live on. Instead of taking responsibility for their lives, find better employment or pursue higher education, they make excuses or blame others.

Straw spelled backwards is **Warts**. Warts are a sign of **problems or stress**. It's like having leprosy. You can almost tell Straw people by looking in their face and by their lifestyle. Just like a piece of Straw, they can't stand up on their own. Straw feels the need to lean on something or someone for support.

Straw gave up on life. Unfortunately, many people are living like Straw. Straw is not limited to people of a particular age group, ethnicity or gender. Because they surrender to the Wolf without a fight, when Straw people look back over their lives they see few achievements and little happiness.

Remember: Straw has the ability to live their dreams; they just don't try.

A Straw Story

Tony and I were classmates in elementary school. Just like other kids he had dreams of being rich and famous and being chauffeured in a stretch limousine. Academically he was an average student but played sports better than all of us. In fact, at the age of eleven, he was already playing basketball and baseball after school with the guys from the local high school team.

By the time we started middle school he was known in the neighborhood for his athletic ability. Most people expected him to at least play college sports if not in the major leagues or the NBA. After graduating from middle school, I went to Thomas Edison High School and he to Brooklyn Technical.

Years later while a cop on Times Square I heard someone call out my name. When I turned around there was Tony. Surprised and happy to see him, I gave Tony a hug. On the corner is a fast food restaurant so we went there to talk and have breakfast.

He informed me that he quit high school in the tenth grade. The work was too hard. Then he started working nickel and dime jobs and fixing cars while he hustled on the street. The more I looked at him the more I could see the pain and regrets in his eyes. Staring at the ground, he said to me, "In my next life, I'll make it."

Oddly enough, I had just recently bought a used car that I was having trouble with. After sharing my problem with him, he told me to meet him with the car that afternoon in front of the restaurant. When I arrived, he revealed he didn't have the proper tools but he believed he could fix the car anyway. Two hours later the car was purring like a kitten. It probably hadn't run that well since it left the factory. After paying him, I gave him my phone number to stay in touch. I figured I could refer him some business and we could reminisce about our childhood. He never called.

A few months later, while visiting friends in the old neighborhood, I saw Tony again. I told him that the owner of the car dealership said that mechanics like him are hard to come by. Few people could have fixed my car without a computer and especially in only a couple of hours. This time I gave Tony the owner of the car dealership's phone number and told him I would even drive him there. No call once again.

At the writing of this book I happened to see Tony's mother. She said that she didn't understand what happened to Tony. Because Tony wasn't focused in school his grades were failing and instead of studying he just gave up. Foolishly, he thought he could quit school and get picked up by a scout while playing street ball. That didn't happen. Then he didn't want to re-enroll in school or go to a trade school. He said the process was too long and he didn't like classrooms. Tony's mother was very hurt to see her son lose out in life and not use his talents. His mother and I have both witnessed Tony's incredible ability to master whatever he chose to do. The only one who didn't see his abilities and opportunities was Tony.

There are Tony's everywhere. Some stand on street corners day after day. No plans, feeling hopeless and helpless. Some work for low wages, earning barely enough to survive and are usually victims of their past choices regarding education, friends or lifestyles. Like everyone, past choices may have put them where they are, but it's their mind-set that's keeping them there. You do have a choice.

Remember: There is no next life. It's now or never.

Wood People

Wood People

The Wood person settles for mediocrity. Wood is straddling the fence between knowing how to live their dreams and wanting things to come easy. Wood is half Straw and half Brick. Most of the time Wood is not satisfied with the success they do have because they are capable of achieving more, but settled for less.

In school, Wood people are under-achievers. Woods settle for a C grade when they are capable of a B or maybe an A. Their schoolwork does not reflect their abilities. They just want good grades; not the best they are capable of.

Teachers describe Wood students as not living up to their potential. They usually aren't disruptive or excessively absent from school. Wood people tend to be struggling with maturity and are typically followers not leaders.

On teams or at work, Wood people do just enough to stay on the team or to not get fired. They say things like, "It's not my job" or "I would but." Wood see others getting promoted and achieving extraordinary success and want the same for themselves but are hampered by their Straw side.

Most people are Wood. They see the benefits that a little more effort will bring and are capable of reaching their goals or dreams but fall short. Wood people understand the consequences of their choices but make excuses for themselves. In fact, Wood tries to show the world their Brick side while hiding their Straw side. Doing this places limitations in their life. They avoid taking leadership positions or getting too involved in activities for fear that others will discover their Straw side.

Wood spelled backwards is **Do** and **Ow**. Wood **knows what to do** to live their dreams but **want to avoid the pain** and discomfort of sacrificing to reach their goals. Instead, Wood people feel the pain later in life knowing that they settled for less. They know if only they had sacrificed, they would have achieved their goals.

Wood people give in. They have dreams, plans and abilities but detour off the path. They typically earn average incomes; their things to do lists are rarely complete and they tend to have a lot of unfinished business.

Wood people have the most regrets in life because there is nothing worse than knowing you could have been more and achieved more but didn't. And the only reason is you!

Remember: A chain is as strong as it's weakest link. For Wood it's their Straw side.

A Wood Story

It was graduation day and I was selected as the Keynote Speaker. As I mingled among the students prior to the ceremony, I heard a lot of graduates talking about their experiences, hopes and dreams. One student sat in the auditorium with tears in her eyes. Her name was Victoria. I sat with her and asked what was wrong. She said that she didn't get accepted to her college of choice. Instead she would be attending her last choice.

Victoria knew what school she wanted to attend. She even took a trip there while in the eighth grade to look at the campus and meet with the admissions counselor. She was even given the school's admissions criteria. What bothered her was that she might have easily been accepted to her first choice if she had applied herself.

Victoria always set goals and was very ambitious. She was involved in the martial arts and music. When she started study-ing karate at the age of ten, her goal was to become a black belt. She studied until the age of fifteen, when she quit as a brown belt, just one belt from black belt. Her reason for quitting; she formed an all girls band and wanted to record a single and try to get a record deal.

Victoria even managed to convince a recording studio to write a song and also record her group for free. She told them she would give them referral business in addition to a percentage of whatever money she earned if the single came out. Then one day she just stopped showing up to recording sessions citing other responsibilities.

And when it came to school, Victoria didn't consider certain classes important, so she did just enough to make sure she got a passing grade. What she didn't consider was that these classes would affect her grade point average and her conduct would be reflected as well. She thought she would have been able to get accepted into her first choice because she excelled in everything else and that she would be able to convince the school to over-look the rules.

Victoria was capable of attaining her black belt but didn't because she quit too soon. She negotiated a great recording deal but doesn't even have a finished record to show for it. In fact, the other members of the group finished the record without her. And when it came to school, she knew what was expected but still slacked off.

Victoria had only been half committed to achieving her goals or else she would have achieved them. The only person Victoria can blame is herself. Victoria is like most people. They know how to accomplish what they want and are fully able. They can even have the path to success in writing but still fall short. Even when they do have some success they can't fully enjoy it because they are constantly trying to hide their shortcomings and are aware of the fact that they could have achieved more.

Remember: It's not enough to know what to do; you still have to do.

Brick People

Brick People

The Brick person plans their life. Brick understands there is no substitute for success. They are fully aware of the Wolf; in fact they have encountered him before. Brick people are aware that the people you invite into your life can bring the Wolf with them. Brick people choose their friends and associates carefully. Usually choosing other Brick people.

In school, Brick people are the achievers. They are the students who plan their study time and do their best. Being Brick doesn't necessarily mean that you get the highest grades in class but it does mean you are doing the best that you are capable of. It is possible to be an average student and still be Brick.

Brick people can be found at all levels of the corporate and work environment. Regardless of their position at the company or on the team, they bring value to the organizations they are part of. Brick people find ways to give more than what they are paid for. They take pride in what they do because they know their work reflects who they are.

Brick people are willing to re-educate themselves, seek out new and creative ways to achieve their goals and understand the value of teamwork. They manage their time and money while focusing on needs and not wants.

Brick people don't look back over their lives with regrets or disappointments. They use life experiences as lessons and stepping-stones. Brick people know that if you don't learn from the past, history will repeat itself.

Brick people never give in to the Wolf. They are the happiest and most successful of the three personality types. Brick people finish what they start and are usually the highest wage earners. Both their personal and professional lives are balanced and successful. Brick people have conversations about success and achieving extraordinary dreams. They look forward to waking up in the morning and accomplishing their goals. It is no wonder that Straw and Wood run to Brick people when they have problems.

Remember: Brick people follow through and finish what they start.

A Brick Story

Carlos Santiago was born in South America and was raised there until the age of thirteen when his family relocated to the United States in search of a better life. Though Carlos didn't speak English, he didn't want to lose time waiting for the school system to teach him.

Being raised in another country and experiencing an unstable government and extreme poverty, Carlos was not going to let anything stop him from achieving his goals. After school he volunteered in the school library putting books on the shelf. He used that time to learn English by reading book titles and by completing basic paperwork.

He borrowed English-speaking cassette tapes from the library and listened to them in his headphones on the way to and from school. One of the cassettes he listened to was on financial planning. Though he didn't fully understand all the terminology he didn't let that stop him. Instead he started keeping a journal and used a dictionary. Then he started listening to tapes on starting a business and on different careers. With these, he also kept a journal.

When it came time to attend college he was already bilingual. Having mastered the Internet, he located college scholarships and various grants, which he applied for and received. With the money he earned working weekends at the grocery store he started a savings account. With part of his money he started a business. The business closed a year later. Then he started three more and they too closed. Finally, after four attempts he found one that worked. Using his life experiences he started a tutoring service for Spanish speaking students where he taught English, basic business courses and money management.

I met Carlos in Miami, Florida while I was there receiving a business achievement award. Carlos was receiving multiple awards. As they read his biography, I looked around expecting to see him walk up to the front. He didn't. He rolled up to the front of the room in a wheelchair. Carlos had lost both of his legs at the age of four due to his family not having money for medical care.

Carlos is not disabled; only his legs are. Disability begins in the mind. Carlos had a dream and was not willing to fail. He made a promise to himself that he would never let anything or his condition stop him from success. If he started something, he would finish it to the end. Having experienced tragedy and poverty he learned from them. He didn't expect things to come easy but he knew that if someone else did it and others wrote about it then it could be done.

You can overcome any obstacle. Every person has challenges. Manage your life so that you don't become your biggest obstacle.

Remember: Anyone can start; it takes a winner to finish.

Who's afraid of the Big Bad Wolf?

As I mentioned earlier, the Wolf confronts all of us. Whether you're Straw, Wood or Brick you will face challenges and obstacles in life. The Wolf can be defeated. But first you must plan and prepare before he is knocking at your door.

When the Wolf couldn't blow down the Brick pig's house he entered through the chimney. The chimney is a metaphor for your brain or thoughts. Preparing for the Wolf, the Brick pig placed a pot of water over a fire destroying the Wolf. If the Brick pig let him dwell inside his home, the Wolf would have destroyed him from inside. Do not internalize a problem. If you do, it will cause stress and will prevent you from achieving your goals.

As a man thinketh he is. When you control a person's mind, you control the person. By allowing a problem to dwell inside you, it will preoccupy your thoughts, actions and attitude. The way you handle obstacles and challenges affects every area of your life, your future, your career, your happiness and your success. Deal with a problem immediately and effectively by planning and preparing. As you go through challenges, grow through them. Some of life's greatest lessons occur during times of trials and tribulations.

Following are ten of the most common Wolves you will experience in your life's journey. There are others but failing to prepare for these Wolves will bring more wolves to your doorstep.

Interesting note: Over 78% of the Earth is made of water and over 90% of our bodies are made of water. So Earth and us are like two bodies of water. And as such we should flow easily together. Life is a mirror image of your choices. Flow spelled backwards is Wolf. When your life isn't flowing and you feel stuck or challenged, you are more than likely facing a Wolf.

Remember: Preparation is the first step to victory.

Wolf #1 — FEAR

Fear is probably the most common Wolf that you will face. Fear can be caused by a variety of reasons, some of them real but most of them created in your mind. Most of us fear that we will not succeed at a given goal or task. The fear of not succeeding has two major side effects. One is that you can become almost paralyzed and withdraw emotionally. The other is that you avoid starting or quit before finishing. Sometimes, the fear is that you might succeed and the responsibilities that come with it.

The key to overcoming fear is to keep in mind that ninety-five percent of the things you fear don't actually happen. Separate feelings from reality. Do things that reinforce your confidence. Recall a time when you were afraid of pursuing a goal but you tried and succeeded. In the case of a new job or career, remind yourself that if you were not capable of doing the job then you would not have been given the opportunity. Opportunity comes to those who are able. It is you who decides if you are ready and willing.

In any new experience there is a learning curve and you should leave room for mistakes. Repeat to yourself, "I can, I will, I Am, if someone else has done it, it can be done." "I earned and deserve this opportunity."

No matter what happens, you will have learned something new. Everybody has fears. It is the person who gives into fear that becomes a victim to it. If fear wins, you lose. Use fear to motivate you.

Remember: You can either live your life or live your fears!

"Your Ears Create Fears"

Stop listening to other people. They do not determine your future. Many times other people contribute to our fears by focusing on the negative. Fear is an emotion that you can either use to motivate you or to deter you.

Since I was six years old, my dream was to become a New York City Police Officer. I was excited when at the age of sixteen; I became eligible to take the exam. Just prior to the test date, some friends and family of mine were talking to me about the dangers of police work and described the Police Academy as a military boot camp. At first, I ignored their comments, but the more I heard, the more convinced I became that perhaps the job wasn't for me. I almost changed my mind.

Fortunately, I decided to take the exam in spite of the fears that everyone was projecting on me. When I received my test score, to my surprise, I achieved a 98.3 on the exam, placing me in the top 1% of the 15,000 test takers.

On January 20, 1987, at the age of twenty, I started the New York City Police Academy. Without a doubt, attending the Police Academy and the experience I gained as a Police Officer has helped me to develop into the person I am today. In fact, even though I left years later to pursue entrepreneurial opportunities, I still say that next to being a Consultant and Speaker, being an Undercover Police Officer was the best job I ever had.

If I had listened to other people then I would not have lived my childhood dream nor would I have met my wife Liz. I met her while I was on duty in midtown Manhattan.

Remember: You don't have to be fearless. Just fear less.

Wolf #2 PROCRASTINATION

Procrastination is putting off things for later when you should be doing them now. Procrastination is as detrimental to success as fear. Most of us know when we are afraid; it consumes us, sometimes speaking to us in our subconscious. Procrastination is the silent killer. Most people procrastinate and don't realize it.

Procrastination can be caused by a multitude of factors. One is perfectionism. Instead of starting or completing a project, the perfectionist is always working on it. If you are waiting for perfection, you will never be finished because nothing will ever be perfect. Stop looking for perfection. Do the best you can and move on. There are other goals you need to start on.

Then there are people waiting for the right time. There are times that are better than others, but studies show that the longer you wait, the less likely you will do something. If you plan on starting a business, taking a new position, furthering your education or any other major life change, consider the cost of waiting and not doing it right now.

Some procrastinators purposely do not prioritize their time and resources to avoid pain or displeasure. Think of the pleasure you will gain from reaching your goals and the pain you will experience if you don't reach them. Start now.

Organize your time and resources by order of importance and challenge yourself to complete your goals. Set deadlines. Deadlines will keep you on schedule and serve as a gauge of how focused and committed you are.

Ask someone you respect to keep you on task. Send them a list of your goals and time-lines. Have them e-mail or call to remind you of the pending deadlines. Place the list on your computer, refrigerator or mirror as a daily reminder.

Reward yourself for completing on time by buying yourself something special. Penalize yourself for not completing on time by not buying something you want until you are finished.

Remember: There are no rewards until you finish, so get started today!

"Maximum Effort, Yields Minimum Risk"

If you want to reduce your risk, put more time and energy into reaching your goals. You become more familiar with the pitfalls and the solutions. A primary reason for people failing to reach their goals is because they procrastinate and do not commit enough time to them. Experts become experts by investing time and becoming competent at what they do.

If you want to fail, then put forth little effort and procrastinate. How can you expect to succeed if you don't spend time trying to succeed? You get out of life, what you put in to it and you can't wait until tomorrow to do it.

When in school, study as much as you can for as long as you can. The difference between the A student and the C student is usually how much time and effort they give to their studies.

I've learned that the people who make the most money in business do research about the business in which they are investing, understand the marketplace, look at the future business climate and maximize their creativity, thus limiting their risk factor. Most importantly, after gathering all of the facts and information to make a decision, successful people make their decisions quickly and without hesitation.

There will always be risk pursuing any goal. The key is to limit the risk by gathering enough information to make intelligent decisions and avoid procrastinating.

Remember: Successful people make up their minds quickly and change them slowly.

Wolf #3 **EXCUSES**

Most excuses are disguised as explanations. Excuses do not pay bills, bring joy nor do they offer opportunity. We all fall short of completing our goals and some of our responsibilities from time to time, but do not take comfort in excuses.

Excuses tend to blame other factors such as your age, ethnicity, time, resources, interruptions, obligations, abilities or others. Unfortunately, none of these are real barriers. Committed people find a way. If you are continuously making excuses, you need to decide how important your goals are. To determine if they are important and critical to making you more successful, write them down on a piece of paper. Draw a line down the page and write on one side "Wins" and on the other side "Losses." Write down what you will gain by accomplishing your goals and what you will lose if you do not. Keep in mind that your "wins" and "losses" extend beyond this particular goal.

As mentioned earlier, your life is the sum total of all decisions made. Your future will be affected negatively if you settle for excuses. And it will be affected positively if you develop the strength of courage and character to make things happen. The easier it is for you to take comfort in excuses, the more excuses you will make and the less successful and happy you will be. Don't settle for excuses, the people counting on you will not and you should not either.

Remember: Excuses are a curse to your goals.

"It's Not What You Don't Have, It's What You Think You Need, That Stops You From Succeeding Or Being Happy"

Many people don't start a business, pursue their goals or apply for a new job or position because they think they don't have enough money, education, experience or contacts. If you appreciate what you do have and maximize your resources, then you will discover that you already possess what you need to get started and in many cases succeed. Most people you meet in life are not aware of what you have or don't have. It is you who reveals this information.

An example of this is when my friend April applied for a job in the marketing department at a large entertainment company. She submitted her application and was called in for an interview.

Though April was nervous and really didn't have a lot of experience in the industry, she didn't want her fears to be an excuse for her not pursuing her goals. During the interview, she told the recruiter why she wanted to work with the company and the value that she could bring to the organization.

After the interview, some of our friends pointed out to April that she did not have any contacts or experience in the entertainment industry. When I began to see the hesitation and doubt appear in April's eyes from what our friends were saying I stepped in. I explained to them instead of focusing on what April lacked, we needed to focus on what she has; extensive life experiences, a degree in a related field, a strong ability to do research and an incredible amount of success in other areas of her life.

When April was hired, all of our friends now had a story about a time when the odds seemed stacked against them. They too remembered that when they focused on their strengths and not their weaknesses they achieved their goals too.

This had been one of my greatest challenges when I was younger. I focused on what I didn't have and thought that I was not qualified to even apply for a job. Many times I had seen someone who had less education, experience and resources than I had, succeed in areas that I didn't think I could have succeeded in. I talked myself out of my own goals. It wasn't until I changed my mind-set and stopped making excuses did things change for me.

We tend to overestimate what it takes to win and underestimate our abilities and resources. In fact, once you get started, every-thing you need seems to fall into place. But first you have to stop finding excuses not to do something and find reasons why you can and should.

Remember: You paint the picture people see!

Wolf #4 **DOUBT**

Doubt or uncertainty happens when you are unsure of your abilities. Doubt can be caused by a lack of confidence due to past experiences, limited education or a lack of familiarity. If you think you are not capable of succeeding then you will think like a failure. Your thinking affects your actions. When you start acting like a failure, you will become a failure because you stop trying and stop looking for solutions.

Winning starts within. You must believe you can do something in order to achieve it. Within each of you lies the power to accomplish almost anything you set your mind to. If a lack of education is the cause, then seek it out. Learning is a never-ending process. Don't let education stop you. If you think education is expensive, time consuming or hard, try ignorance.

Some doubters think they need to wait on others for support or approval. Waiting on others denies you the opportunity to learn and to take pride in accomplishing your goals. Furthermore, you probably will never begin. If you absolutely do not know what to do, then seek assistance. There is nothing wrong with asking for help. It takes courage to be humble.

Push past the doubt. Keep working towards your goals. With

each step you will develop more skill and confidence. Focus on finishing your immediate and short-range goals first. As you see yourself making progress, you will become more effective, more powerful and more determined to succeed.

Remember: If it is to be, success is up to ME.

My Expectations.
My Education.
My Endurance.
My Effectiveness.
My Enthusiasm.

"Falling Isn't Failing;
It's Part Of The Process"

We all fall when we learn something new, just like when we first learned how to ride a bicycle. But falling happens to everyone. If you don't develop the courage to get up and try again then you would begin to doubt yourself and never learn.

When I started my consulting career, I struggled for years experiencing highs and lows or, as they say in business, peaks and valleys. Every time I found myself in the valley I learned something new. I learned what went wrong and how to avoid falling.

I still remember my first business venture; I quit the first time I had some obstacles. I felt like a failure. Then I discovered that even though the business failed that I was not a failure. Believe it or not, if it were not for the hard times and seeing myself try in spite of the struggles, I probably would not appreciate the good times as much as I do today.

A fall teaches you a lesson. You learn how to find solutions to problems. When you see yourself as a failure, you give up and stop trying because you lose confidence and begin to doubt yourself. I learned that I can fall but I can get back up and win.

Most great achievements or even long term relationships have experienced challenges. There probably would not be any fifty-year wedding anniversaries, medical or technological advances, or successful people if they weren't committed enough to endure in spite of the challenges and obstacles.

Don't be afraid to fall. Everyone falls. With it, come some of life's greatest lessons and opportunities. Use a fall to motivate you to do things differently and better. This is how you learn and come to appreciate your blessings. A fall becomes a failure when you look at yourself and the experience negatively. Falling is not failing; it is part of the success process; in fact the harder the fall, the greater the lesson.

Remember: Don't ask why me. Instead ask what can I learn from this experience.

Wolf #5 CRITICISM

Criticism is one of the main causes for depression and low self-esteem. Criticism can cause pain, fear and procrastination. It can also reduce your confidence as well as have countless other character destroying affects. Separate criticism from good advice. Criticism is meant to destroy or tear down. Dismiss criticism immediately. Even when meant to be helpful, criticism can be harmful and destructive to your self-esteem.

Some people who criticize are trying to cover up their own shortcomings or inadequacies. Don't let other people's problems become yours. Always consider the source and the motive. When pursuing a goal, regard other people's advice in the proper context. They are expressing their own opinion, which does not necessarily make them correct. It's okay and quite healthy to believe that you may have the solution or right answers.

Use advice as a tool to make an honest evaluation of yourself or dreams to see if there are any areas in which you can improve. When you identify areas to work on, improve them, but do not criticize yourself. Be aware that not all criticism comes from other people. Some people are much more critical of themselves than other people could ever be. This is self-destructive. Correct your actions but do not destroy who you are. For everything you need to correct, there are probably a hundred more things that don't need correction.

Remember: Love yourself.

"Don't Take A Poll, Take Control!"

Stop surveying your friends, family and sometimes even strangers before you make a decision. If you have an idea, take the time, do research and decide what you are going to do. There is always more than one way to accomplish a goal. When you survey people by asking for their opinions and suggestions you leave yourself vulnerable to possible criticism.

I'm reminded of author and motivational speaker Les Brown. He tells a story about how he would tell his friends that one day he would be known as "the Motivator." Laughing at him they would tell him to get a job in Sanitation and to forget the Post Office because there you had to take a test. Few people supported him and most criticized his dream.

Many years ago I met Les Brown via telephone through a mutual friend, Michael Gillespie. The reason for the call was that I ordered his first cassette tapes and wanted to thank him. Les Brown did it, in spite of other people's criticisms. And his products were the first motivational tapes I ever owned. It was his story and message that inspired me to do what I do today.

If Les Brown had let criticism hold him back then maybe he wouldn't have pursued his dreams. And maybe I wouldn't be a motivational speaker or the author of this book.

Remember: Don't let criticism stop you from achieving your dreams. Other people may miss out on theirs.

Wolf #6 **DEBT**

Use sound judgment when it comes to your finances. Distinguish between wants and needs. You need clothing, food, shelter and basic transportation. Jewelry, expensive cars and overpriced name-brand goods are wants, not needs.

Contrary to popular belief, material possessions and image is nothing. The most valuable commodity in life you cannot own. Nothing can take the place of having people in your life that you love and respect, and that love and respect you.

In the business world, many people think that they need to look the part to get the part. Many times this is true. Most times though you can creatively look the part without spending a lot of money. Shop at garage sales and thrift shops. Avoid name brands and adopt the attitude that less is more.

Be responsible with your money. When you watch the pennies, the dollars watch themselves. Debt is a major cause of stress and will distract you from your goals. Debt is always easier to get into than to get out of. Following are some tips to managing your money and creating wealth.

- Develop a budget and stick to it.

- Save at least 15 % of your income.

- Avoid using credit cards and applying for too many.

- Pay off all debt as soon as possible.

- Save 4-6 months of expenses in an emergency account.

- Buy a used car instead of a new one.

- Take advantage of all available tax deductions.

- Start a business.

Remember: Any fool can get into debt; it takes a wise person to avoid it.

"Don't Deal With The Branches, Deal With The Roots"

After college a classmate of mine found himself in an incredible amount of debt. Credit card bills were past due and creditors were calling almost daily. His car payments were late and he was struggling financially.

When we met to discuss his situation, I asked him for a list of all of his outstanding debts. Instead of just coming up with a solution for paying off his debts, I examined his spending habits. Writing a check and paying off the debts would not have solved the problem. The debts were the by-products of his not being committed to a budget. A few years earlier, he had a similar amount of debt and his solution was to pay them off without examining the cause.

Because he dealt with the branches, the debts, and not the root of his credit problems, which was his lack of discipline, the debts reoccurred. Now when he has a problem, he digs deeper and tries to find the real cause of the problem and make the proper adjustments.

Whenever you are facing a major challenge, look at why and how the problem began. When you learn to make better decisions, you will reduce the amount of challenges you will face. You are responsible for most of the things you experience in life whether it is pleasant or unpleasant. Take responsibility for your life.

Remember: When resolving a problem, you have to get to the root or origin of the problem.

Wolf #7 COMPETITION

Don't let competition stop you from pursuing your goals. Don't take your employer, clients or family for granted. There is always someone out there who wants what you have. Never think that you are indispensable. No one is indispensable.

Your worth to a company is based on the amount of service you give. They may pay you by the hour, but they are not paying for your time; you are paid for the amount and quality of service you give.

Competition means that your dreams are worth pursuing and that others see the value as well. Use competition to motivate you to be the best you can be. Competition is what makes champions reach beyond their grasp and accomplish feats previously unheard of. Competition is a major catalyst for progress. Without competition, inferior products and incompetent labor would be the standard. Learn from your competition. Find out what skills or abilities they possess and emulate them.

Give more than what is expected of you and more than what people are accustomed to receiving. Build strong relationships. Relationships give you the edge and lead to lasting friendships. Respect the people in your life and they will respect and be loyal to you. Competition means you have to continue to educate yourself and appreciate your blessings or someone else will.

Remember: Compete with yourself to always do better next time.

"Don't Focus On Success, Focus On the Steps And Success Will Follow"

Success is a process. You earn a degree only after taking each of the required classes one at a time and passing the necessary examinations one question at a time. If you focus on competing with your classmates and try to take too many classes in one semester then you probably will not succeed.

While I was in school, some of my classmates were more concerned with having the degree than mastering the skills. They wanted the degree instantly. Unfortunately for them, they did not want to accept and respect the process and quit before graduating.

There is a saying, "You can pay me now or pay me later." This saying is especially true when it comes to education. Take the time to learn the skills necessary to achieve your degree or certificate and don't concern yourself with the actual paper. The paper or diploma will come when your part is done, not before.

The same is true for starting a business. If you concern yourself with becoming a multimillion dollar company more than focusing on ensuring that your company is properly structured and is growing one customer at a time, you'll lose your business before you get started. A company grows one customer at a time just like graduating from school happens one class at a time.

Anything worth working for will not happen overnight. The key to achieving any goal is to identify what is needed, the order they need to happen and focus on doing first things first. The key to building a house is to build it one brick at a time. There is less stress when you focus on the steps rather than the competition or the finished product. This way you get to celebrate your successes along the way. If you set unrealistic goals or unrealistic time frames to accomplishing your goals, you will give up.

Remember: The key to success is like walking. Just put one foot in front of the other.

Wolf #8 TEMPTATION

You only have twenty-four hours in a day. If you subtract eight hours for sleeping, four for eating and other necessities, one-and-a-half for travel and eight hours for work or school, you only have two-and a-half hours per day for yourself. How you use these hours is critical.

Use your time effectively by organizing your day and prioritizing your responsibilities. Temptation will cause you to sacrifice needs to obtain wants. Don't be tempted by outward appearances. Develop discipline and self-control. Don't give into lusts and wants. Learn to tell yourself no. Temptation will distract you from your goals and dreams.

A feeling of guilt usually accompanies giving in to temptation. The guilt is your conscience chastising you for failing to exercise self-discipline. Lack of self-discipline will lead you down the wrong path. Weigh the cost of temptation. If it is not part of your larger plan, leave it alone.

Be true to yourself. Accepting the truth shall set you free from temptation and unnecessary distractions. Don't compromise and sacrifice your future for temporary satisfaction. Your goal is permanent happiness and success.

Remember: Life is like mathematics. A straight line is always faster than a crooked one. Do not detour.

"Success Comes From Sacrifice, Sacrifice From Self-Discipline, Self-Discipline From Self-Awareness"

When you are aware of who you are and what you want out of life, you see the benefits of self-discipline. The more disciplined you are, the easier it is to resist temptation and sacrifice your time and resources to reach your goals.

It takes a mature person to understand and apply this quote to their life. But once you do, your life changes instantly. Self-awareness is accepting the truth about yourself, your strengths, and your weaknesses. It is impossible to exercise self-discipline if you do not know yourself. You are the most important person when it comes to achieving success or happiness in your life.

Some people do achieve some level of success without self-awareness. We have all heard about these people. They seem to have everything, but are unhappy and experience bouts of depression, and are tempted to heal their pain through drug and/or alcohol abuse. After obtaining material possessions, fame or prestige, they discover who they really are and what they really want out of life. Unfortunately for them, neither money nor fame can buy happiness. They must begin the process of resisting their temptations in order to achieve their true happiness.

I have had my greatest success and happiness when I take the time to get to know myself better. This is why I spend so much time meditating, to increase my own sense of self-awareness.

Remember: Know Thyself.

Wolf #9 YOUR PAST

Your past is not your future. Don't judge yourself based on past choices or experiences. We all make mistakes and will continue making mistakes. The key is to learn and grow from those experiences. Don't let your past cripple you. Forgive yourself.

The same is true for past successes. Don't become complacent or arrogant. Always remain humble. Life doesn't make any guarantees, nor does it play favorites. It is never too late to succeed and it is never too late to turn success into failure. Use past experiences as stepping-stones. Learn yesterday's lessons, but leave yesterday in the past.

Avoid self-pity. Self-pity is a very powerful and destructive force. It leads to discouragement, defeat and pain. Move on. Today is a new day and with it come new challenges and opportunities that need your undivided attention. You cannot move forward looking backwards, if you do, you will stumble and fall.

Remember: Just like the past, your future will be decided based on the choices you make today.

"If You Do Not Have The Power To Change Yourself, Nothing Will Change Around You"

The things you experience in life are a result of the choices that you make. If you want to change what you are experiencing or going through, you need to change yourself. The events in your life as well as the people in your life, reflect the decisions you are making. Until you change yourself, the reflection will not change.

You cannot wait on conditions to improve first. You must take control of your life. Other people can give you advice, but it is only you who can make the difference in the quality of your life.

Decisions divide your life into two, before the decision and after. Make sure that after is better than before. By the way, choosing not to make a decision is making a decision.

It's about personal accountability. You have to accept responsibility for your life. It would be foolish of you to expect your life to change if you do not change first. So many people sit around complaining about their condition in life and refuse to take action. They go around telling everyone the same story day after day hoping someone else fixes the problem. These people are the least satisfied with their lives. Things won't change until you accept the fact that you are responsible for your life, not anyone else.

Remember: Everything starts and ends with you!

Wolf #10

LACK OF SUPPORT

Not everyone will believe in your dreams. This includes friends and family members. One of the greatest challenges to pursuing your dreams is trying to convince others to agree with or understand your dreams. Unless you need their support or resources, it is usually best to not share your plans with too many people. Most people cannot see beyond their own circumstances or goals. Do not expect them to understand yours.

For some of you, a lack of family support could lead to family problems or a deferment of your dreams. Evaluate your goals and find a way to identify any areas that might be causing the disagreement. Make sure your dream isn't selfish, unrealistic, dangerous or harmful to others. Share your goals with your family detailing objectives, time-lines, expectations, and the benefits. Be sure to express your desire for their love, support and encouragement.

Your family is no different than other people; they too sometimes cannot see beyond their own circumstances or dreams. Make sure you maintain effective communication. Communication is key to effective relationships.

Surround yourself with people who will support, encourage and guide you. To have a friend, you must first be a friend. Be a friend by supporting others who are also trying to achieve their dreams.

Remember: You cannot wait on support. It usually comes after you start, not before.

"When You're Ready, A Mentor Will Appear"

When you're ready, a mentor does appear. When you experience this, you develop the courage to work on your goals even when it seems that the odds are not in your favor. Once you get started, help seems to come from everywhere. Successful people like helping other people become successful. When you want something bad enough, you send energy out into the world that you are looking for a mentor and one finds you.

Don't try to accomplish everything at once. Look at what you want to achieve and divide it into little pieces. Complete what's necessary. Do the most important things first.

There will be times when you will want to start something new but don't have the experience. But once you start, you will begin to think and act differently, while creatively looking for solutions and opportunities. It is during these times that you begin to attract to you and find the resources that you need. Mentors find you when they see you are taking responsibility for your goals.

Remember: Don't worry about needing help, help will find you.

Seven C's of Success

The Seven C's of Success

In this section, we will discuss the qualities that Brick people possess. I refer to them as the Seven C's of Success: Character, Commitment, Confidence, Competence, Consistency, Creativity and Courage. Anyone can learn and apply them to their life. As I mentioned earlier, being Straw, Wood or Brick is a choice.

It has been said that insanity is doing the same things over and over again expecting different results. For some of you, the quote may sound familiar, for others, you have just discovered that you have been acting insane. None of you would buy seeds that couldn't grow. So why would you settle for a life that is stagnant? With change comes growth. Growth cannot happen without change. If you want to change your life, change your mind-set. Your mind-set affects your attitude and your attitude affects your actions.

Just like at the end of *The Three Little Pigs*, after Straw and Wood saw the benefits of preparing for the Wolf and being Brick, they too built Brick houses. Mastering the Seven C's will lead you to Brick, allow you to defeat the Wolf and achieve happiness and success in life and business.

Remember: Your life reflects your choices. Choose to Master the Seven C's and become Brick.

Character

"The ultimate measure of a man is not where he stands in moments of comfort, but where he stands in time of challenge and controversy." **Rev. Dr. Martin Luther King, Jr.**

The most important quality a person can possess is Character. Character comes from a person's spirit and soul. It is like the reservoir from where all your decisions come from. If you lack Character you will find yourself making decisions that will lead you down a Straw path. Character is about integrity, honesty and morality. A developed Character possesses self-control and achieves respect from others.

Commitment

"The quality of persons life is in direct proportion to their commitment to excellence, regardless of their chosen field of endeavor." **Vince Lombardi**

Commitment is the giving of you to your word and aspirations. Commitment helps you to develop endurance. When you're Committed you don't waiver, unsure of your decisions. Achieving your goal is your priority. Because you have totally given of yourself, you will want and expect the very best possible outcome. A lack of Commitment creates chaos, hesitancy and doubt. When others see you are Committed they work to help you make it happen.

Confidence

"Clear your mind of can't." **Samuel Johnson**

Confidence is belief in your self, your abilities and possibilities. Confidence begets enthusiasm. Confidence says try and try again. Confidence knows no limitations and seeks solutions. Confidence is the backbone of self-esteem. Without Confidence your self-esteem is shattered and you will give up before even trying. Confident people are unstoppable. They may fall down but they get up and keep trying.

Competence

"Skill comes from doing." **Ralph Wardo Emerson**

Competence is more than being capable. Competence is excelling. Being Competent is only achieved by doing. Watching may make you familiar but you will not develop skill. Competence is what separates the amateur from the professional. Competence is usually achieved only after a series of failed attempts and carries with it an invaluable ability to resolve problems. The more Competent you become the more valuable you are to you, your family and society.

Consistency

"A half-hearted goal may get you half way to where you want to go... but I doubt it. It's more likely to get you just as far as the first detour, and off you go in another direction."
Alec Mackenzie

Consistency is continuous effort. Consistency is necessary to achieve any goal. Inconsistency stops progress. Consistency is to life like the wheels are to a bicycle. Once the wheels stop the bicycle falls. Unless you are Consistent your efforts dilute over time making them ineffective and in vain.

Courage

"Courage is not the absence of fear, but rather the judgment that something else is more important than fear."
Ambrose Redmon

Courage is personal power. Your life grows or shrinks according to your Courage. Courage sees beyond fear and sees the possibilities. A lack of Courage means a life of hopelessness. When you display Courage the rest of your body, mind and spirit follows. Courage goes beyond your comfort- zone seeking new skills and experiences.

Creativity

"The "how" thinker gets problems solved effectively because he wastes no time with futile "ifs" but goes right to work on the creative "how." **Norman Vincent Peale**

Creative people are problem solvers. Life offers no blueprint for success or happiness. If you're not Creative, you'll find yourself stuck or having to pay others for solutions. Creative people live out of their imaginations. Life is a dynamic changing place. As life evolves solutions must also evolve. Creative people are always in demand.

Remember: The Seven C's of Success: Character, Commitment, Confidence, Competence, Consistency, Creativity and Courage.

Brick Building Blocks To Success And Happiness

1. How you think is critical to your success. Be **Confident**. Focus on success not failure. Avoid negative people and environments.

2. Have clearly defined goals and dreams. Be specific and create a plan of action to achieve them.

3. Develop **Courage**. A dream without action is nothing. Don't let anything stop you. Take custody of your life.

4. Educate yourself. Read. Acquire new skills. Be **Competent** at what you do.

5. Be **Committed** and **Consistent**. Life is a voyage, set your sails for traveling the distance. Never give up!

6. Analyze details. Gather facts. Do not leave any stones unturned.

7. Plan your time and money. Do not be easily distracted. Do not settle for mediocrity or failure.

8. Be **Creative**. Be different. Be a leader not a follower. Be you.

9. Effective communication is essential to effective leadership. Listen to and inspire the people around you.

10. Accountability. Everything starts and ends with you. If you fail to develop your **Character** you will discover that you are your greatest obstacle and steps 1 through 9 will not matter.

Final Thoughts

Research shows that over 80% of the World's population are not up to their potential. It's not for a lack of information, in fact we are deluged with information. Unless you are living your dreams or exceeding your expectations for your life, then you are among this group. You only have one life to live. Don't settle for less than you deserve.

You are born a winner. In order to live the life of a winner you must think and act like a winner. This does not mean you will not face obstacles. Even Brick faces obstacles. What it does mean is that you must learn how to effectively deal with obstacles and challenges. If you truly want to achieve success in life and business, it is not enough to apply only some of the C's. You must master and apply all of them on a regular basis. Develop the power of belief. Defeat disbelief and the negative power it creates. Visualize yourself achieving your goals and your mind will work to make it happen.

Some people say, "I can," they only acknowledge they have the ability to achieve their goals but don't act on them. Others say, "I will," they acknowledge their abilities and then defer for a later date or time, which usually never comes. Brick People say, "I AM." They acknowledge their abilities and decide to do it now. They claim their goals and dreams. Brick people make things happen. Learn to make things happen.

Your mouth holds the key to your destiny. Use your words to change your world. Encourage yourself. If you use negative words, you will reap negative results. Use positive words. Count your blessings. Pray and meditate daily. Confess with your mouth the things you want and desire out of your life. Let the world know that you are confident and are committed to achieving your dreams.

Lastly, listen to your life. It will tell you what direction you are heading in. If the sound of your life is growing fainter and fainter amidst the noise and constant howling of the Wolf, you are heading in the wrong direction. Turn around. You can make different choices. You are not obligated to continue following the path that you are on.

Remember: Don't let a Wolf stop you from living your dreams. Prepare for the Wolf.

About Robert Roots

Robert Roots, a former NYC as well as Coral Gables, Florida Police Officer, is a successful entrepreneur, Consultant, Speaker, Writer and Personal Success Coach. His expertise has been retained by both large and small organizations.

A respected consultant, he was retained by the 4th largest school district in the country, Miami-Dade County Public Schools, to design and author a training manual for teachers and administrators. The manual, *"The Career Day Guide,"* positively impacts almost a half a million students and school personnel annually.

Due to his dedication to educating youth and young adults about the dangers of drug and alcohol abuse, he was tapped by the U.S. Coast Guard to star in their national television campaign aimed at educating the public about the dangers of drug and alcohol abuse.

Robert is proud to be a product of the New York City School System where he is an alumni of John Jay College of Criminal Justice and a graduate of P.S. 171, I.S 145 and Thomas Edison High School. In addition, he credits the success he has had in life to the Boys Clubs of America, the Martin DePorres Center, the Cub Scouts and Boy Scouts and the Tae kwon do Martial Arts school that he was a member of in Queens, New York.

Determined to make a difference and touch millions of lives,

Robert Roots has made it his life mission to inspire others and to be proof that it does not matter where you come from.

Robert Roots shares four children, Robert, Janara, Michael and Emmanuel with his beautiful and supportive wife Liz.

For more updated information, please go to:

www.RobertRoots.com

Thank you.

Contact Page

It is always a pleasure to hear from people who have read, **"Prepare for the Wolf."** If this book has added value to your life or someone you know, please write and let me know. I would love to include your story in my next book or on my web site.

If you would like for me to speak at your organization or are interested in purchasing additional copies of this book or other products, please do not hesitate to contact me at: **RR@RobertRoots.com**

I look forward to hearing from you soon.

For more information, please view my web site:

www.RobertRoots.com

Resource Guide

The following are excellent resources for your personal and professional growth and development. For a complete description of these books and magazines, please go to your local bookstore or your local public library.

Magazines

Black Enterprise Magazine
1-800-727-7777
www.blackenterprise.com

Business Week
1-800-635-1200
www.businessweek.com

Entrepreneur Magazine
1-800-274-6229
www.entrepreneur.com

Money Magazine
1-800-633-9970
www.money.cnn.com

Success Magazine
1-615-844-0184
www.success.com

Time Magazine
1-800-843-8463
www.time.com

U.S. World News and Report
1-800-436-6520
www.usnews.com

Books

Art Of The Deal, The - Donald Trump

Don't Sweat The Small Stuff - Richard Carlson, Ph. D.

Greatest Salesman in the World, The - Og Mandino

How To Speak Like A Pro - Leon Fletcher

It Only Takes A Minute To Change Your Life - Willey Jolley

Lead The Field - Earl Nightingale

Live Your Dreams - Les Brown

Magic Of Thinking Big, The - David J. Schwartz, Ph.D

Making College Count - Patrick S. O'Brien

One Day My Soul Just Opened Up - Iyanla Vanzant

Books *Cont'd*

Prophet, The - Kahlil Gibran

Releasing Your Potential - Dr. Myles Munroe

Rich Dad, Poor Dad - Robert Kiyosaki / Sharon Lechter

Road Less Traveled, The - M. Scott Peck

Science Of Personal Achievement, The - Napolean Hill

Speaking To Excel - James Amps

9 Steps to Financial Freedom - Suze Orman

Succeeding Against The Odds - John H. Johnson

Think And Grow Rich - Napolean Hill

Unlimited Power - Anthony Robbins

You Can Make It Happen - Stedman Graham

Notes

Notes

Notes

Notes